Mysteries OF THE PYRAMIDS

© Aladdin Books Ltd 1995

Designed and produced by
Aladdin Books Ltd
28 Percy Street
London W1P 0LD

First Published in the United States by
Copper Beech Books, an imprint of the Millbrook Press
2 Old New Milford Road
Brookfield, Connecticut 06804

The author, Dr. Anne Millard, has a Ph.D. in Egyptology from University College, London. She is the author of numerous books on ancient Egypt and other aspects of the ancient world.

The consultant, George Hart, is an Egyptologist working at the Education Section of the British Museum, London. He has written extensively on ancient Egyptian books and pyramids.

Editor: Katie Roden
Design: David West Children's Book Design
Designer: Flick Killerby
Picture Research: Brooks Krikler Research
Illustrators: Francis Phillipps,
Stephen Sweet: Simon Girling and Associates, Rob Shone.

Printed in Belgium

Library of Congress Cataloging-in-Publication Data
Millard, Anne.
The Pyramids / by Anne Millard.
p. cm. -- (Mysteries of --)
Includes index.
ISBN 1-56294-938-1 (lib. bdg.). --
ISBN 1-56294-194-1 (pbk.)
1. Pyramids--Egypt--Juvenile literature. [1. Pyramids--Egypt.
2. Egypt--Antiquities.] I. Title. II. Series.
DT63.M516   1995   95-13269
932--dc20   CIP   AC

Mysteries OF THE PYRAMIDS

Anne Millard

Copper Beech Books
Brookfield, Connecticut

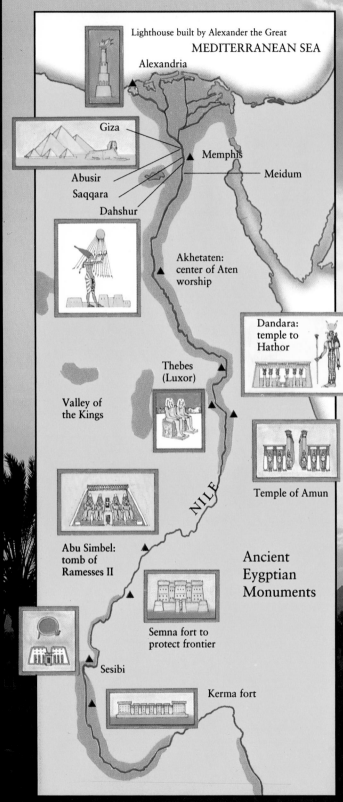

Lighthouse built by Alexander the Great

MEDITERRANEAN SEA

Alexandria

Giza

Memphis

Abusir

Saqqara

Meidum

Dahshur

Akhetaten:
center of Aten
worship

Dandara:
temple to
Hathor

Thebes
(Luxor)

Valley of
the Kings

Temple of Amun

NILE

Abu Simbel:
tomb of
Ramesses II

Ancient
Eygptian
Monuments

Semna fort to
protect frontier

Sesibi

Kerma fort

CONTENTS

" The sky is overcast,
The stars are darkened,
The celestial expanses quiver,
The bones of the earth-gods tremble,
The planets are stilled,
For they have seen the King appearing in power..."
(Beginning of Pyramid Text no. 273)

Introduction to
THE MYSTERIES

They stand silent and mysterious on the Giza Plateau in Egypt – three mighty pyramids and six smaller ones. Meanwhile, across the world, vast pyramidlike structures tower above the rainforests of Central and South America – monuments of great empires which now have disappeared.

There are more than three dozen kings' pyramids in Egypt, but as time passed, all knowledge of their royal history was lost. People came up with some weird ideas, believing that the pyramids were anything from ancient observatories to the work of visitors from outer space!

It was not until the nineteenth century A.D. that the pyramids were examined in great detail. Since the age of the first explorers, lots of puzzles have been solved, but modern science still cannot explain many unanswered questions. In the last few years, a French and a Japanese team have both claimed to have evidence that there are other chambers in the Great Pyramid at Giza, unopened since the days of Khufu over 4,000 years ago. What secrets might these chambers reveal? Will they help us to understand the great civilization of ancient Egypt?

"To take a better footing we put off our shoes and most of our apparel, foretold of the heat within, not inferior to a stove. Our guide went foremost, everyone with our lights in our hands. A most dreadful passage...not above a yard in breadth and four foot in height...so always stooping and sometimes creeping." (seventeenth-century English explorer)

The First
EXPLORERS

If you visit a pyramid today, you will find electric lights, steps to climb, and handrails to help you find your way. When early explorers entered 300 years ago, they had only flickering candlelight and the strong hands of their guides to lead them into the intense heat and fearsome darkness of the pyramids. There was a terrible stench, and the air was dusty. But the explorers braved the heat and lack of light, and had many adventures!

The first tourists to visit the Giza pyramids were the ancient Egyptians themselves, then the Greeks and Romans. After the Arab invasion of Egypt in A.D. 639, the outer stones from the pyramids were used to build the city of Cairo. For centuries after, very few people visited Egypt, so scholars had very little information about the pyramids. Were these wonderful monuments just tombs? Surely they must have had other uses?

Early Explorers
AND DISCOVERERS

Throughout history, people have tried to understand the pyramids. Early Christians thought they were places where priests watched the stars. In the nineteenth century, some people believed that the measurements of the Great Pyramid were devised by God, and that from them they could predict the future! But by then, scholars could read ancient Egyptian writing and they had started to dig up ancient sites. The pyramids were finally known as the last resting places of Egypt's ancient kings.

A SENSITIVE APPROACH
Sir William Flinders Petrie (1853-1942) is regarded as the father of modern archaeology. He dug sites carefully, recorded everything in detail, and published his results. His first job in Egypt was to measure the Great Pyramid.

EARLY ADVENTURER
Jean de Thevenot (below) was one of the first explorers of ancient Egyptian sites.

THE BURIED SPHINX
In Egyptian legend, the Sphinx (the statue which guards the pyramids) appeared to a prince in a dream. It promised to make him king if he cleared away the sand covering its body. He did so, and became Tuthmose IV.

NAPOLÉON'S NIGHTMARE
Napoléon Bonaparte, the Emperor of France, led an invasion of Egypt in 1798. Legend has it that he ventured into the Great Pyramid alone, only to emerge pale, shaken, and gasping for air. What secrets did he encounter in the darkness? We will never know...

TREASURE HUNTERS
In the early nineteenth century, great damage was done by collectors and their agents. They entered the tombs in all kinds of ways, including blasting their way in! Giovanni Belzoni was a former circus strongman who was hired by a collector to gather ancient Egyptian artifacts. He had no idea of preservation – one of his writings describes how he clumsily crushed Late-Period mummies as he forced his way into a tomb.

Preserving the treasures
Many museums and universities have carried out excavations in Egypt. The objects found are treated by experts, then stored for future research. X rays, medical scanners (below), robot photography, and many other modern techniques are used to help scientists understand the secrets of the tombs.

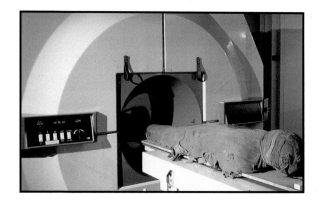

PYRAMID GRAFFITI
Belzoni even carved his name on the stones of the pyramids!

When did tourists start to arrive? In 1869, Thomas Cook, a British travel agent, bought a steamboat in Egypt and offered a new service – a package vacation. He charged one price to cover everything – travel to Egypt, a cruise along the Nile, and a guide. Until then, visitors to Egypt had to arrange all these details for themselves, which could be both difficult and extremely expensive.

UNCHARTED TERRITORY
After the Arab invasion of Egypt, few people were able to visit the country. Little was known about the pyramids, the Nile valley and its surroundings, or the culture and history of ancient Egypt.

Reading the HIEROGLYPHS

The Egyptians had invented a picture writing that we call hieroglyphs by about 3000 BC. Some of their signs were single letters; others had the value of two, three or more letters. These were combined to form words. Hieroglyphs take a long time to write, so the Egyptians invented a "shorthand" script which we call *hieratic*, and another, *demotic*, about 2,500 years later. These were used in daily life, and hieroglyphs were kept for religious texts only. For centuries, no one could read the hieroglyphs, but in 1822 a great breakthrough was made...

THE ROYAL CARTOUCHE

To emphasize and protect royal or holy names, the Egyptians wrote them in a frame called a cartouche (above). Champollion (see below) used cartouches on the Rosetta Stone to help him translate the hieroglyphs. He read the one below in its Greek version. It was Ptolemy, a ruler of Egypt. He then worked out which hieroglyphs spelled the name.

P		L		Y	S
T	O	M			

FINDING THE KEY

The Rosetta Stone is carved in hieroglyphs, demotic and Greek. It was discovered in Egypt in 1799.

* *no translation*

	i	y	y	*
*				

w	*	b	p	f

m	n	r	h

h	kh	h(soft)	s	s

sh	q	k	g(hard)

t	tj	d	dj

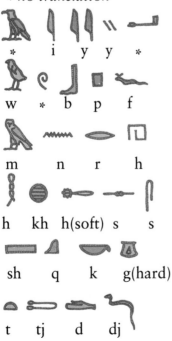

CRACKING THE CODE

In 1822, a brilliant young French scholar, named Jean François Champollion, used his knowledge of ancient Greek to read the Rosetta Stone. At last, the mysterious hieroglyphs could be translated.

ΠΟΜΕΙΝΛΖΔΑΠΑ
ΛΕΝΛΚΑΙΟΧΥΡΠΕ
ΧΘΕΙΣΙΝΕΙΣΛΥΤΛ

NEW TEXTS

The last hieroglyphic inscription was carved in Philae temple in AD 394. Old Egyptian writing then died out. Instead, people used an alphabet called coptic. The name comes from an Arabic word, gubti, based on the ancient Greek name for Egypt.

A letter in demotic script.

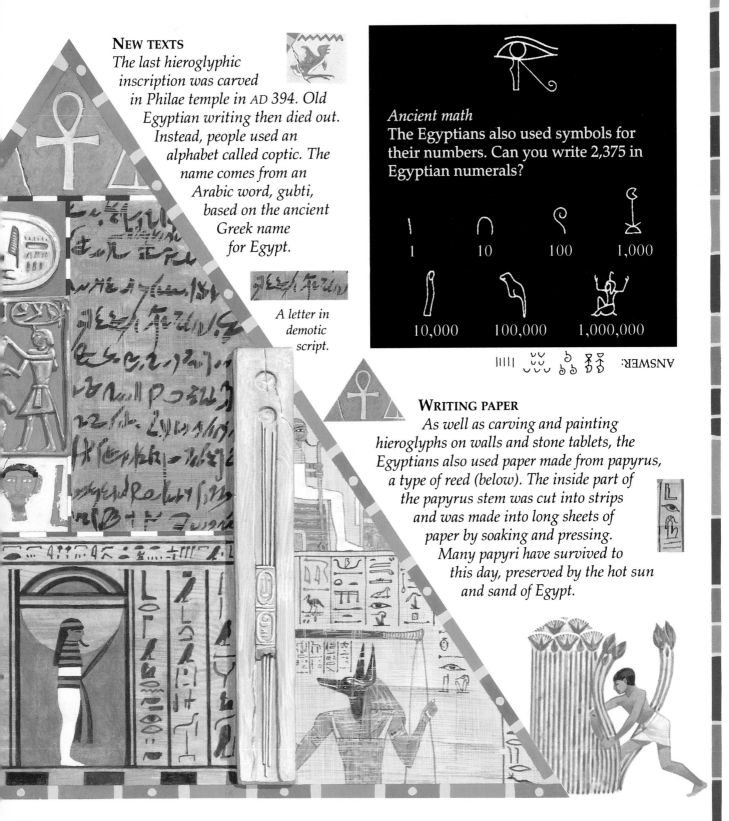

Ancient math
The Egyptians also used symbols for their numbers. Can you write 2,375 in Egyptian numerals?

1	10	100	1,000

10,000	100,000	1,000,000

ANSWER:

WRITING PAPER

As well as carving and painting hieroglyphs on walls and stone tablets, the Egyptians also used paper made from papyrus, a type of reed (below). The inside part of the papyrus stem was cut into strips and was made into long sheets of paper by soaking and pressing. Many papyri have survived to this day, preserved by the hot sun and sand of Egypt.

HEAVENLY GUIDE BOOKS

In the pyramid of the last king of Dynasty V and in all Dynasty VI pyramids, we find writings called the Pyramid Texts. These were believed to help the king move easily into the Next World (heaven).

They contained prayers, pleas, and ritual pronouncements to the gods. It was hoped that the gods, such as Anubis (left), would welcome the King and allow him to pass into the next world to live a new, happy, and everlasting life.

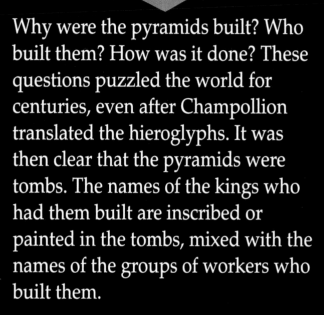

Building the PYRAMIDS

> "The fashioner of costly stones seeks for skill in every kind of hard stone. When he has fully completed things, his arms are destroyed and he is weary. When he sits down at the going in of Re [sunset], his thighs and his back are cramped."
>
> The Satire of Trades

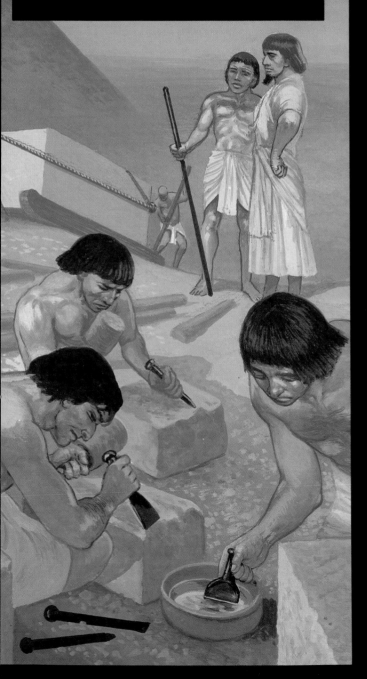

Why were the pyramids built? Who built them? How was it done? These questions puzzled the world for centuries, even after Champollion translated the hieroglyphs. It was then clear that the pyramids were tombs. The names of the kings who had them built are inscribed or painted in the tombs, mixed with the names of the groups of workers who built them.

Most Egyptian people were farmers. Egypt had very little rain, but water was supplied by the Nile. Every year the river flooded, covering the land for four months. During this time, the *Inundation*, the farmers could not tend their fields, so the king summoned them to work on his pyramid instead. This labor was a form of tax to the king. People usually went willingly, although the work was hard. They believed that the king was a god and would look after them in the next world in return for their labor.

Construction AND LABOR

When a suitable firm site had been chosen, the ground was flattened and the base of the pyramid was sketched out. Building could then begin. The great stones were tied to sleds and dragged into place one at a time by a team of workers. Finally, a white limestone casing was put on the pyramid.

BUILDING BLOCKS
Most of the stone for the pyramids came from local quarries, but the fine white limestone for the casing (right) came from Tura on the east bank of the Nile, and had to be floated across the river. Each block was then put on a wooden sled and dragged into place by a group of workers. To help the sled run smoothly, the workers put wooden rollers on the ground in front of it. Water was poured continuously onto the rollers, so that the heat and friction caused by the movement of the enormous stone would not start a fire.

THE CONSTRUCTION SITE
Even straight-sided pyramids were built with a step pyramid inside them (top). To build the central structure, the stone blocks were probably dragged into place up ramps made of bricks and rubble (center). One wide ramp (bottom) was used to add the outer casing. It was made longer and higher as the pyramid grew taller, and was taken apart when building ended.

How many blocks made a pyramid?
This depended on the size. The Great Pyramid contains about 2,300,000.
How much did each block weigh?
This also depended on size. Most Great Pyramid blocks were about 2.5 tons.

THE HOLY ARCHITECT
The designer of the first pyramid was named Imhotep. In about 2700 B.C., he built a step pyramid for King Zoser. He was so wise, and his pyramid was so impressive, that he was later worshipped as a god!

The pyramid complex

On the edge of the complex was the Valley Temple, which was probably where the king's body was prepared for burial. A causeway (path) led to a Mortuary Temple, where offerings were made to the king's spirit. There was also a small pyramid for the queen and rectangular tombs, or mastabas, for the royal family and the courtiers.

Mortuary Temple

GLEAMING WHITE
Originally, the pyramids were covered with fine white limestone (above). However, over the centuries this was stolen.

Causeway

Valley Temple

A HUGE WORKFORCE
Skilled stone masons, laborers, and other craftspeople worked all year round on the pyramids, but most of the work was done during the four months of the Inundation, when the farmers arrived to do their labor tax. They were fed, housed, and clothed by the king. It was an enormous feat to look after so many people – as many as 80,000 at one time – and to organize their work efficiently! The workers were paid in beer, oil, and linen. They also received food including meat, fish, vegetables, fruit, cheese, and a type of wholewheat bread.

TOOLS OF THE TRADE
The Old Kingdom pyramid builders had copper chisels and saws, and wooden sleds to pull the blocks. To carve the blocks from the quarries, wooden wedges were driven into the rock and soaked with water. The wood swelled, splitting the stone. Another method was to heat the rock then throw cold water over it, to make it crack.

Pyramids AND KINGS

Egypt's kings were believed to be related to the gods and were treated with great respect. At first they were buried in rectangular brick tombs. But Imhotep decided that mud did not last long enough for royal burials, and built a stone mastaba for his ruler, Zoser. He made it bigger by putting another mastaba on top, then another, and another...and the world's first step pyramid was born. King Huni built another step pyramid, but his son Sneferu made its sides straight.
From then on, all pyramids were built with straight sides.

GREAT MONUMENTS
The biggest and best-built pyramids are those at Giza. They belong to three kings of Dynasty IV (c. 2575-2465 B.C.) – Khufu, his son Khafre, and his grandson Menkure. Khufu's is the Great Pyramid, but Khafre's looks bigger because it was built on higher ground and still has some of its limestone casing. In the tombs were figures of servants (above), to look after the king.

A MAGICAL SEND-OFF
Around Zoser's pyramid (below) were many solid buildings. His spirit passed through them by magic.

THE ROYAL GRAVEYARD
The smaller, less well-built pyramids at Abusir and Saqqara belong to the kings of Dynasties V and VI. These sites are packed full of tombs, dating from throughout the Egyptian period. The tombs include the pyramid of King Userkaf (right), with a colossal head of the ruler.

18

Did the builders ever make mistakes?
The pyramid builders were usually incredibly accurate, down to the last inch. But everyone makes mistakes! King Sneferu built two pyramids at Dahshur, one of which is known as the Bent Pyramid. It was meant to have straight sides, but when it had been partially built, the architects decided that its sides were too steep and it might collapse. It was therefore finished with the sides sloping more gently at the bottom, so it looks bent.

A COMPLETE DISASTER
The Meidum Pyramid was the engineers' biggest blunder! At some point, all the outer casing fell off, dragging most of the insides down with it. Sneferu's engineers made a mistake – they built the new, straight-sided casing on soft sand instead of rock.

The Bent Pyramid at Dahshur.

Zoser (right), a god-king of Egypt.

A class of its own
The Great Pyramid is unlike any other pyramid, with three main chambers rather than one. Were these last-minute changes of design to trick grave robbers? The highest chamber is the only burial chamber, where the king lay.

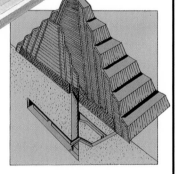

The Great Pyramid at Giza.

A step pyramid layout, with an underground burial chamber.

The lower one is called the "Queen's chamber," although the queen was buried in her own small pyramid. There are four tiny shafts in the king's and queen's chambers. Many people think they were built to help the royal spirits reach the stars. Most other pyramids are simpler, with one central burial chamber and two or three antechambers.

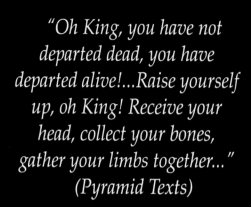

"Oh King, you have not departed dead, you have departed alive!...Raise yourself up, oh King! Receive your head, collect your bones, gather your limbs together..."
(Pyramid Texts)

A Life after DEATH

The Egyptians believed that the only way they could properly enjoy life in the next world was if their bodies survived. Even the king's body had to last, in case he needed it, although his soul traveled to the next world to live with his godly relatives.

In Egypt, people had been buried in shallow graves in the hot desert sand. This dried and preserved the bodies in a natural way. However, once the Egyptians put their kings and nobles in splendid tombs, the bodies decayed easily, and artificial ways of preserving them were invented. The most successful method – mummification– was at its peak in the New Kingdom. The internal organs (lungs, brain, liver, etc) were taken out and the body was covered with a salt called *natron*, which dried it out. It was then stuffed with linen and resin (the sap from trees), and wrapped in hundreds of yards of linen bandages. Many bodies are still almost perfectly preserved today.

Preparing for THE AFTERLIFE

It sometimes seems that the ancient Egyptians spent most of their time thinking about death, but this isn't true. They loved their life on earth so much that they believed the next world would be like Egypt, but without sadness, worries, or suffering. They therefore went to great trouble to prepare for their eternal life and make sure they would have a good time. This meant building a comfortable tomb, full of all the furniture and belongings they might need. Over all, they made sure they would have regular supplies of food, drink, and entertainment.

SOULS AND SPIRITS
The Egyptians believed they had three spirits – the ka, ba, and akh. The ka was the life force of a person. After death it lived in the tomb, and was kept comfortable with offerings and servants. The ba represented the personality. It was shown as a human-headed bird, but it could change shape and leave the tomb. The akh, written as a crested ibis, went to join the stars, or Osiris.

MEMORY AIDS
Mummies were decorated with an image of the dead, so the ba recognized the body. Mirrors and combs enabled the dead to look their best.

HEAVENLY PLEASURES
Paintings of food and entertainers (below) were often placed in a tomb, to keep the souls happy.

Why are mummies called mummies? The Arabs thought bitumen was used in embalming, so called mummies after their word for bitumen, "mummiya."

WEALTH AND RICHES
Jewelry and treasures were usually put in the tombs of both men and women. Even the poorest people were buried with some jewelry, to make sure they looked impressive in their new life with the gods and goddesses.

HEAVENLY SERVANTS
Little servant figures, or shabtis (right), were put in the tombs to do the dead person's work in the next world.

Grave robbers
Everyone knew that great riches were placed in royal tombs. While guards watched over the burial places, these treasures were safe. But over the centuries the tombs were no longer guarded, and thieves broke in – even though they knew it insulted the gods. If they were caught, they would be executed, but this did not keep them away!

LONG LIFE
The organs were preserved and put in containers called canopic jars.

SAILING IN THE SKY
In some dynasties, model boats were placed in the tombs. They represented the boat that carried dead people across the Nile to the next world.

Full-sized boats have been found in several tombs at Giza. They were probably used by the king in life, and to carry his dead body across the Nile to his final resting place.

Joining the G O D S

In the Old Kingdom, the chief god was the sun god Re, who sailed across the sky every day in a boat. His children were Tefnut (Moisture) and Shu (Air). They were the parents of Geb (Earth) and Nut (Sky), whose children were Osiris, Set (the lord of desert and storms), Nephthys his wife, and the stars. Set murdered his brother Osiris, cut up his body, and threw the pieces into the Nile. Isis and Nephthys gathered up the pieces and brought Osiris back to life, with the help of Anubis. When a king died, he went to the heavens to join the gods.

WEIGHING YOUR CHANCES
Anubis (below) was the guardian of the dead. He held the scales of justice. People had to prove that they were worthy of entering the Kingdom of Osiris (above) by having their heart weighed against the Feather of Truth (above). If the scales balanced, a person had a good life. An evil heart would tip the scales and they would be thrown to a terrible monster, the Devourer.

IMAGES OF THE GODS
Gods like Geb (bottom center) and Shu (above right) were believed to have beards. Kings, and queens if they ruled as kings, wore false beards to show their closeness to the gods.

Which deity had the most power? Isis, the loving mother of all, had more magic power than any other god or goddess. In ancient Roman times, her fame spread outside Egypt – evidence of Isis worship has been found as far north as Hadrian's Wall, in England, built about A.D. 120.

Sacred pets

The Egyptians wanted to be close to their gods and goddesses, but no living person was allowed to look at them. Therefore, people chose a special animal or bird for each deity. The spirit of the god or goddess would enter the body of the creature, and so could be near his or her worshippers and bring them comfort. Cats were especially popular, and many animals were mummified like their owners.

HORUS

Horus, the son of deities Isis (right) and Osiris, fought his evil uncle Set (below), then went on to become the King of Egypt. In the desperate fight with Set, the left eye of Horus was plucked out. The eye of Horus became the symbol of sacrifice and of offerings to the dead. The moon was also believed to be Horus' left eye. Horus was usually portrayed as a falcon (left) in traditional ancient mythology and art.

TEMPLE WORSHIP

Huge temples were built as homes for the gods and goddesses on earth. Only priests, priestesses, and royalty could enter the temples; ordinary people worshipped at home. The deity's statue was kept in a shrine, and brought out daily to be cleaned, dressed, and worshipped with prayers.

"A stairway to the sky is set up for me that I may ascend to the sky..."

"May the sky make the sunlight strong for you, may you rise up to the sky..."

(Pyramid Texts 284 and 523)

New Ideas and INVESTIGATIONS

The pyramid was the place where the king's body and possessions were buried, and where offerings were supposed to be made to him forever. But it was also the place where the god-king's spirit was launched to the heavens to join his relatives, the gods and goddesses.

Most experts agree that the souls of the early kings were believed to be heading for the stars. Step pyramids were stairways to the stars, and straight-sided pyramids were like sunbeams made of stone, which the king could climb to reach Re.

But the pyramids may have had many more uses. Does the pyramid also represent a mound, which in Egyptian creation stories was the first land to appear from the original nothingness? Does the layout of the Giza pyramids imitate the position of the main stars that form the belt of the groups we call Orion and Sirius? How can we explain several missing mummies and empty tombs?

Secrets of
THE STARS

The movements of the sun, moon, and stars were important in Egyptian religion, and their calendar was based on these movements. Each week was marked by a new group of stars rising in the sky at dawn. The Egyptians divided the stars into constellations (groups), but their groupings were different from ours. Maps of the heavens show the sun god and the stars crossing the sky in boats. This shows how important the Nile was to the Egyptians.

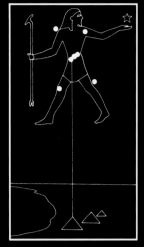

MAPPING THE STARS
The group of stars we call "Orion" was known as "Sahu" by the Egyptians. They believed that the soul of Osiris went there after he was murdered by his evil brother, Set. Near Orion is the star we call Sirius, known to the Egyptians as Sopdet. They saw Sopdet as Isis, the wife of Osiris. Sopdet spends seventy days a year below the horizon, invisible from Egypt. Its return marked the Egyptian New Year. The Nile flood came at the same time, and was believed to be Isis weeping for Osiris.

STARRY GODS
Many temples were decorated with constellation gods (right) and star deities.

HEAVENLY BIRDS
In the Old Kingdom, swallows were identified with the stars. They heralded the dawn, and were often shown on the front of Re's sun-boat. In later images, the head of a falcon was shown descending from the sky. It represented the sun's rays, and the eye of Horus.

HOLY COW
The cow (right) was the sacred animal of the goddess Hathor, the Queen of Heaven.

How did the Egyptian calendar work? The Egyptian week had ten days. Three weeks made a month and twelve months a year. There were five holy days at the end of the year, making 365 days in all.

THE SACRED SKY
The sky hieroglyph (above) shows the heavens as a solid ceiling, and was often used above doorways.

A VIEW OF THE WORLD
The sun was believed to be the right eye of the god Horus.

THE LOVE OF THE GODS
The Egyptians believed that the sky was the goddess Nut (below), stretching her body over the Earth. In Egyptian mythology, Nut married Geb, the earth god, but Re was against the marriage and ordered their father, Shu, to push them apart. However, by this time Geb and Nut were already the parents of the stars and the four great deities.

Mysteries of the heavens
What are the four narrow shafts that lead out of the burial chambers in Khufu's pyramid? Recently, it was discovered that one of the two shafts in the king's chamber points to the northern stars, which never sink below the horizon. The other points to Orion. Was this a passage for the dead king's soul to reach Osiris quickly? It is also suggested that the queen's chamber shafts point to the stars. One faces Sirius – could this be another passageway to the heavens?

Orion/
Sahu/
Osiris

Sirius/
Sopdet/
Isis

The Giza pyramids are not quite in a straight line. The Egyptologist Robert Bauval claims they are laid out like the three brightest stars of Orion.

THE DIVINE STARS
The northern stars were always visible, so they were named "The Imperishable Ones."

Puzzles and MYSTERIES

In the Middle Ages (1100-1500 A.D.), the pyramids were said to have been grain stores, then were believed to be early observatories. In the nineteenth century, one theory said that the Great Pyramid's measurements were inspired by God and contained a code that could predict all the main events of world history! Even today, crazy ideas about the pyramids are still popular, but new evidence and theories are constantly improving our understanding of these great, mysterious monuments.

A SECRET CHAMBER?
In 1994, a team of scientists sent a tiny robot, called UPUAUT II, up the narrow southern shaft of the queen's chamber of Khufu's pyramid. They wanted to see if they could ventilate the pyramid better, because of the numbers of tourists visiting it every year. The robot traveled about 200 feet...then its TV camera showed a slab of stone with copper handles blocking its way. What lies behind this tiny door? Could there be a room? What might it contain – a statue, hidden writings, wonderful treasures... or nothing at all? Archaeologists are hoping to look through a crack at the base of the stone with a tiny camera, the kind used by doctors to see inside patients. What will it reveal?

AN ANCIENT PUZZLE
Archaeologists believe that the Sphinx was carved from stone left in a quarry when the pyramids were completed. But there is a theory that it is thousands of years older than the pyramids, because the wind and rain have worn away its face much more than the surface of the pyramids. It is believed that the Sphinx was the work of an earlier civilization. This is extremely unlikely because no other traces of such a civilization have been found.

EXTRATERRESTRIAL EGYPTIANS
There are even people who suggest that the pyramids were built by aliens!

THE CASE OF THE MISSING MUMMY

When excavators entered the unfinished step pyramid of King Sekhemkhet, the stones blocking the passage were in place, a wreath of flowers was still on the coffin and the lid was sealed. Excitedly, they pried it open, and found...nothing! What had happened to the body? Had it been buried secretly somewhere else, to fool robbers? Had it been stolen? Or had it never been buried at all? So far, the mummy has still not been found, and it is unlikely that it ever will. It seems the pyramids will present us with new puzzles and mysteries forever.

Hi-tech research

In recent years, science and technology have helped archaeologists to unravel many of the mysteries of Egypt. There are many ways of dating human and animal remains, wood, and pottery. X rays have been used to examine mummies for many years, and modern medical scanners can give an even better picture of what is inside them. This is very important, unwrapping a mummy can often destroy it. Artists and computers can reconstruct the faces of people who lived 3,000 years ago.

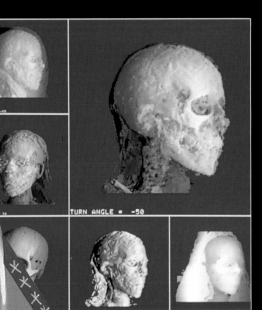

TURN ANGLE = -50

How did the Egyptians look ? Archaeologists use police techniques

to recreate mummies, faces from ancient skulls, with clay.

"The usual method of sacrifice was to open the victim's chest, pull out his heart while he was still half alive, and then knock down the man, rolling him down the temple steps which were awash with blood."
(José de Acosta, 1590)

Pyramids around THE WORLD

The Egyptians were not the only civilization to build great pyramid-shaped structures. The ancient peoples of Mesopotamia (now eastern Syria, southeastern Turkey, and most of Iraq) built pyramid shapes to bring them closer to their gods and goddesses. They constructed mud-brick platforms, with temples to house the gods on the flat tops. There the priests sent offerings and prayers to the gods. We call these temple platforms *ziggurats.*

In North, Central, and South America, people such as the Aztecs and Incas also built flat-topped pyramids (left). People were sometimes buried under them, but they were not meant to be tombs. Temples were built on top of these pyramids, where sacrifices of food, animals, and sometimes human beings were offered. Early Native American peoples built large, pyramid-shaped mounds in which to bury their dead and to use as shrines.

P o p u l a r PYRAMIDS

Central and South America saw the rise and fall of many civilizations, such as the Olmecs, Toltecs, Maya, Incas, and Aztecs, before the arrival of European settlers in the sixteenth century. These people first built great mounds of earth, then developed flat-topped pyramids by casing the mounds in stone with steep steps. These were places where gods and people could meet. The pyramids had temples on top, but some had burials underneath. The Europeans destroyed hundreds of ancient cities, and many treasures and artifacts were lost.

SACRIFICE AND CEREMONY
To please their gods, the Maya offered their own blood at special ceremonies. Sometimes they also offered human lives. The Aztecs believed that their many gods needed human hearts to stay strong, and sacrificed thousands of people to them. Sacrifices were made before shrines on flat-topped pyramids, such as that at Tikal in Guatemala (right). Picture writing has been found on some Mayan pyramids and is being translated.

INCA PYRAMIDS
The Incas ruled a vast area of South America in the fifteenth century. In the city of Cuzco in Peru they built a great temple, Coricancha (right), for their sun-god Inti. There they offered food and beer and sacrificed animals to their god.

THE MODERN MONUMENT
A glass pyramid (right) is the entrance to the Louvre Museum in Paris.

Did other people mummify their dead?
Mummification is a very old practice in South America. Mummies of the Nazca people in Peru date from about 200 B.C. to A.D. 500. Human sacrifices were sometimes buried in the Andean mountains, where they were naturally preserved in the snow and ice.

REMEMBERING THE DEAD
Stone or ceramic funeral masks were used in the funeral rites of several Native American cultures, similar to those of the Egyptians.

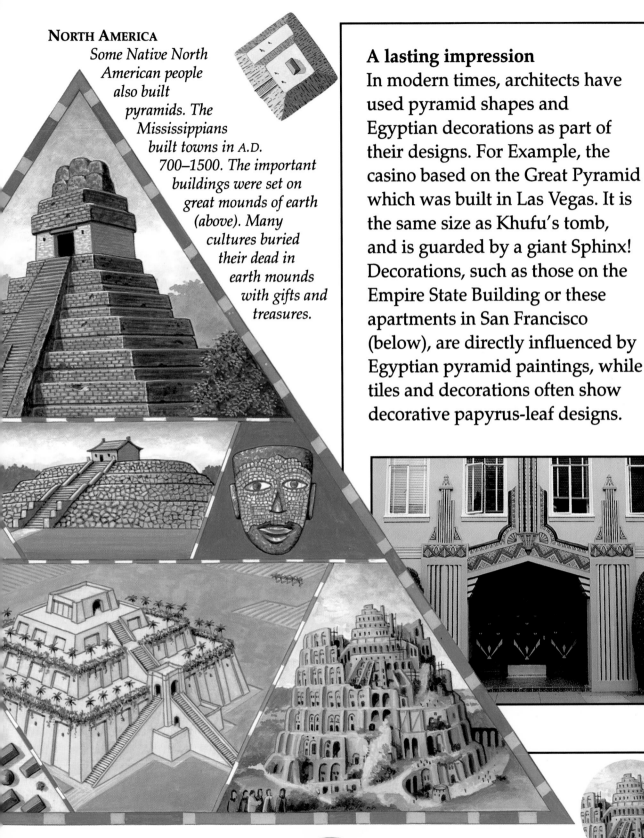

NORTH AMERICA

Some Native North American people also built pyramids. The Mississippians built towns in A.D. 700–1500. The important buildings were set on great mounds of earth (above). Many cultures buried their dead in earth mounds with gifts and treasures.

A lasting impression

In modern times, architects have used pyramid shapes and Egyptian decorations as part of their designs. For Example, the casino based on the Great Pyramid which was built in Las Vegas. It is the same size as Khufu's tomb, and is guarded by a giant Sphinx! Decorations, such as those on the Empire State Building or these apartments in San Francisco (below), are directly influenced by Egyptian pyramid paintings, while tiles and decorations often show decorative papyrus-leaf designs.

Biblical buildings

The early people of Mesopotamia built mud-brick temples on platforms on the ruins of older temples. The platforms grew taller over the years and became huge, stepped mounds similar to early pyramids.

We call them ziggurats. The great ziggurat Etemenanki was built by King Nebuchadnezzar (630-562 B.C.) in Babylon, home of the famous Hanging Gardens. It might have given rise to the story of the Tower of Babel (right).

The lasting IMAGE

Middle Kingdom rulers also had pyramids, which were usually made of brick rather than stone. People soon realized that pyramids were easily robbed, so the New Kingdom rulers picked a remote valley to hide their rock-cut tombs – the Valley of the Kings, it has a pyramid-shaped mountain towering above it. The workers who cut those tombs built their own village at Deir-el-Medina. All their tombs had mini pyramids on top.

After Napoléon's expedition in 1798, a craze for ancient Egypt began. This happened again after the opening of the Suez Canal in 1869, and in 1922 with the discovery of the tomb of Tutankhamen. Each time, people collected Egyptian antiques and visited Egypt. Others bought Egyptian-style jewelery, furniture, architecture, or ornaments. Egyptian images were used in all sorts of advertisements and packaging – even for products that had nothing to do with Egypt. Today, the pyramid shape and Egyptian decorations are used in many products, from chocolate to makeup.

Is the Great Pyramid great? The sides are 754 feet long, and the height just over 490 feet. The base is so big that you could easily fit eight football fields on it.

36

WHAT WERE THEY FOR?
A mosaic in St. Mark's Cathedral in Venice, Italy, shows how people in the Middle Ages continued to be fascinated by the pyramids. They were believed to be ancient grain stores built by Joseph (of multi-colored coat fame), and were shown complete with doors and windows!

GRUESOME USES
In medieval Europe, many people believed that mummies had healing powers. They ground them into fine powder for medicines. King Francis I, of France, (below) swore by powdered mummy as a tonic! In the nineteenth century, mummy parts were used as ornaments, and mummy unwrappings were social events. Modern cyrogenics allows people to be "frozen" scientifically when they die, in the hope that they can be revived in the future.

Still more to discover?

Despite centuries of exploration and discovery, there are still a great number of mysteries to be solved. Many sites still need to be excavated. Only recently the remains of Khufu's Valley Temple and an ancient bakery were unearthed, and in 1995 an amazing discovery was made in the Valley of the Kings – the rock-cut tombs of several sons of Ramesses II. Every year, there are new ideas and new theories about how and why the pyramids were built. UPUAUT II has shown that there are many undiscovered secrets. How much more is there to find? Will our ideas be proved correct? Whatever happens, the pyramids will continue to intrigue people worldwide for centuries to come.

TIME

c. 5000–3100 B.C. **Predynastic Period**
Upper & Lower Egypt formed

c. 3100–2686 B.C. **Archaic Period
(Dynasties I–II)**
Upper & Lower Egypt united

c. 2686–2650 B.C. **Old Kingdom
(Dynasties III–VI)**
c. 2686–2649 King Zoser
c. 2680 Step Pyramid built
. 2589-2566 King Khufu
c. 2580 Great Pyramid built
c. 2666-2505 Kings Khafre & Menkure

c. 2150-2040 B.C. **First Intermediate Period
(Dynasties VII-X)**
Collapse of rule of the Kings

c. 2040-1640 B.C. **Middle Kingdom
(Dynasties XI-XIII)**
c. 2040 Egypt reunited

c. 1640-1552 B.C. **Second Intermediate Period (Dynasties XIV-XVII)**
Invasion by foreigners called Hyksos; they are later driven out

c. 1552-1085 B.C. **New Kingdom (Dynasties XVIII-XX)**
Kings buried in Valley of the Kings

c. 1085-664 B.C. **Third Intermediate
Period (Dynasties XXI-XXV)**

c. 664-332 B.C. **Late Period (Dynasties
XXVI-XXX)**
c. 525-404 & 341-332 Persians take Egypt

605-562 B.C. *City of Babylon rebuilt*

LINE

332 B.C. Alexander the Great conquers Egypt

323-30 B.C. The Ptolemies rule Egypt

30 B.C. Egypt becomes part of Roman Empire

A.D. 250-900 Maya empire at its most powerful

A.D. 639-642 Arab forces invade and rule Egypt

A.D. 700-1200 North American mound cities built

A.D. 950-1200 Toltecs invade and rule Maya lands

1400s Aztec and Inca empires expand

1500s Spanish take South American empires

1798 Napoléon Bonaparte invades Egypt

1799 Rosetta Stone discovered in Northern Egypt

1817 Giovanni Caviglia opens Great Pyramid

1822 Hieroglyphs translated

1850 Excavation of pyramids at Saqqara

1880-1881 Petrie surveys Giza pyramids

1900-now Excavations at Saqqara & Giza

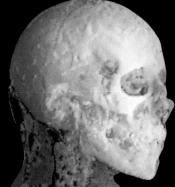

1922 Carter discovers tomb of Tutankhamen

1994 UPUAUT II finds tiny door in Queen's chamber shaft of Great Pyramid at Giza

1995 Rock-cut tombs of several sons of Ramesses II discovered in Valley of the Kings

INDEX